fondue

By Lou Seibert Pappas

Photographs by Alison Miksch

CHRONICLE BOOKS

SAN FRANCISCO

Text copyright © 2005 by Lou Seibert Pappas.
Photographs copyright © 2005 by Alison Miksch.
All rights reserved. No part of this book may be repro-
duced in any form without written permission from the
publisher.

Library of Congress Cataloging-in-Publication Data
available.

ISBN 10: 0-8118-5137-0
ISBN 13: 978-0-8118-5137-0

Manufactured in China.

Design and typesetting by Carole Goodman,
    Blue Anchor Design
Food styling by William Smith
Prop styling by Leslie Siegel
Photography assistance by Jada Voght
Food styling assistance by Matthew Vohr

10 9 8 7 6 5 4 3 2 1

Chronicle Books LLC
85 Second Street
San Francisco, California 94105

Thanks and appreciation to the following for providing
the beautiful cookware and serving ware photographed
for this book: Chantal Cookware Corporation
(chantal.com), Chocolate Bar (chocolatebarnyc.com),
Home & Haven (homehavennyc.com), Jonathan Adler
(jonathanadler.com), La Cafetière (la-cafetiere.com),
Pearl River (pearlriver.com), Williams-Sonoma
(williams-sonoma.com).

Cointreau is a registered trademark of Cointreau
Corporation, Frangelico is a registered trademark of
Giorgio Barbero & Figli S.P.A., Grand Marnier is a
registered trademark of Société des Produits Marnier-Lapostolle,
Guittard is a registered trademark of Guittard Chocolate
Company, Inniskillin is a registered trademark of Inniskillin
Wines, Inc., Kahlúa is a registered trademark of The Kahlúa
Company, Pernod is a registered trademark of Pernod
Ricard, Scharffen Berger is a registered trademark of
SVS Chocolate LLC., Valrhona is a registered trademark
of Valrhona S.A.

www.chroniclebooks.com

ACKNOWLEDGMENTS

What a joy to experience the skilled talents of two Chronicle editors: Laurel Leigh, a creative gem with copy and layout, and Leslie Jonath, a devoted pro in conceiving and managing many book projects. And many thanks, also, to Jonathan Kauffman for the smooth copyediting.

With many thanks to Cathy Priest, a great cook, as well as Sharon Armstrong and Joan Bower, other Kappa Kappa Gamma alumnae friends, for their enthusiastic testing. An additional thank-you to cooking class members Tong Sun Kobilka, Rhoda Daner, Lisa Skinner, and Yiva Risano. And a grateful thanks to Claire Stewart Kostic and Sandy Stewart Stevenson for their inspiration as I crafted menus.

TABLE OF CONTENTS

INTRODUCTION

FONDUES ARE BACK IN STYLE. THIS POPULAR DISH OF THE 1950S AND '60S has been rediscovered for intimate entertaining with flair.

The word *fondue* may derive from the French word *fondre*—meaning "to melt." The French-speaking canton of Neuchâtel in Switzerland is often credited with creating the original cheese-and-wine fondue in the sixteenth century. One legend suggests that the dish originated during fighting between Protestants and Catholics, who reached common ground after the two created a communal dish together, one side providing the bread and the other the cheese. However, mentions of fondue have been found in court records from 1,000 years ago. In fact, a prototype of fondue using wine, goat cheese, and barley can be found in Homer's *Iliad*.

What commenced as a simple Swiss peasant dish, created out of necessity, has spawned countless variations. The fondue repertoire now encompasses vegetable, seafood, and meat fondues cooked in broth or oil, as well as elegant dessert fondues.

These fondues present diners with options that suit the trend toward lighter, more healthful dining. A fondue party can satisfy vegetarians and meat fanciers alike. The cooking medium can be hot, fat-free broth. The wide range of sauces presented with each recipe allows for personal creativity in the menu.

Served on celebratory occasions, fondue creates a special closeness and congeniality as guests share a communal pot and everyone participates in the meal. At holiday times, fondues are ideal. Many families and groups of friends carry on a tradition of serving fondue on Christmas Eve around a crackling fire. Other special occasions include tree-trimming parties, Hanukkah dinners, and New Year's Eve festivities.

A fondue party offers many rewards. It's convivial and distinctive. Preparations are easily made in advance. Hosts cherish being able to enjoy their guests, as the cooking is done at the table. Plus, cleanup is minimal.

You, the host, can design a party around an appetizer, entrée, or dessert fondue—or all three types at a single occasion. Another virtue of fondue menus is that they are adaptable to any time of day.

For decades I have had the fun of savoring fondues. In the 1950s, one of the earliest assignments of my career at *Sunset* magazine was to write and style an article on Swiss Gruyère and Emmentaler fondue (a version appears on page 17). Later I savored the original on the slopes of Zermatt. International travels have broadened my love for this versatile dish and its many offspring. I have featured Shabu-Shabu (page 45), Beef Bourguignonne Fondue (page 40), and luscious chocolate fondues in countless stories.

Friends who married in the 1950s delight in telling tales of the fondue pots they received as wedding presents. Now, as they celebrate their fiftieth anniversaries, they have rediscovered their prize ceramic-and-steel pots for celebratory family soirées. And younger generations are reveling in the ease of plugging in an electric fondue pot for an intimate feast.

As you enjoy the fondues this book inspires you to make, may you dwell in the warmth of this happy custom.

—Lou Seibert Pappas

CELEBRATORY MENUS

Here are some of my favorite menus featuring fondue. The complementary recipes suggested below, while not incorporated in this cookbook, are easy to find in any number of seasonal cookbooks. Or, you can experiment by making up your own menus. Remember, the important ingredient is *fun*!

Adventurer's Fondue Party

Green salad with red grapes and caramelized pecans

Asian Duck and Vegetables in Broth (page 47)
 Sauces: Chile-Peanut Sauce (page 72) and Teriyaki Sauce (page 74)

Syrah or Pinot Noir

Raspberry Fondue (page 93)

Inniskillin ice wine

Mediterranean Dinner in the Garden

Caesar salad

Tuscan Cheese Pesto Fondue (page 29, *variation*)
 Dippers: Mushrooms, artichoke hearts, and bread sticks

Pinot Grigio or Chianti

Pine nut biscotti and espresso granita

One-Pot Family Dinner

Chinese Steamboat (page 48)
 Sauces: Sesame-Cilantro Sauce (page 70) and Chile-Peanut Sauce (page 72)

Sake or Chinese beer

Chocolate-Peanut Fondue (page 85)

Greek Island Party Dinner

Hummus

Stuffed grape leaves

Country salad with tomatoes, cucumbers, and feta cheese

Greek Island Lamb Fondue (page 42)
   Sauces: **Aioli (page 68) and Yogurt Sauce with Mint (page 75)**

Pilaf

Pinot Noir or Shiraz

Baklava and halva

Teriyaki Dinner

Watercress, hearts of palm, and mandarin orange salad

Beef Teriyaki Fondue (page 41)
   Sauces: **Ponzu (page 72) and Sesame-Cilantro Sauce (page 70)**

Steamed white rice

Sautéed sugar peas

Shiraz or beer

Candied Ginger, Lemon, and Cream Cheese Fondue (page 91)

Green tea

Chocolate Lover's Valentine's Day Dessert Party

White Chocolate–Almond Fondue (page 83)

Chocolate-Orange Fondue (page 77)

Cappuccino Fondue (page 80)
   Dippers: **Strawberries, pineapple chunks, banana slices,
   tangerine segments, marshmallows, and pound cake**

Coffee and cappuccino

Seaside Fondue with the Clan

Coleslaw with Fuji apples

Beach Lover's Fish Pot (page 55)

Corn on the cob

Watermelon wedges

Oregon Pinot Gris

Tree-Trimming Supper

Classic Swiss Cheese Fondue Neuchâteloise (page 17)

Green salad with red and gold cherry tomatoes

Crusty French bread

Rhine Riesling or other dry white wine

Apple crisp with Calvados whipped cream

Claire's Christmas Eve Fondue Dinner with Family

Cocktails

Smoked Scottish salmon and cream cheese

Raw vegetables and chips with guacamole

Fresh Dungeness cracked crab and dry sparkling wine

Spinach salad with dried cranberries, slivered almonds, jicama, and raspberry vinaigrette

Filet Mignon and Shrimp Fondue (page 38)
Sauces: Basil Pesto (page 73), Chile-Peanut Sauce (page 72), Tomato Cocktail Sauce (page 67), Dijon mustard, and prepared horseradish

Garlic mashed potatoes with green-onion purée

Cabernet Sauvignon

Chocolate truffles

Hanukkah Dinner Party

Japanese Tempura, Fondue Style (page 60)
  Condiments: **Grated peeled fresh ginger and Ponzu (page 72)**

Spinach and tangerine salad with pistachios

Pinot Gris or Sauvignon Blanc

Almond soufflé cake

New Year's Eve Party

Endive and watercress salad with blood orange segments, avocado, and pomegranate seeds

Scallop, Shrimp, and Fish Fondue (page 57)
  Sauces: **Sour Cream–Dill Sauce (page 67) and Tomato Cocktail Sauce (page 67)**

Jasmine brown rice

Crusty French bread

Champagne

Caramel-Pecan Fondue (page 86)
  Dippers: **Strawberries, banana chunks, pineapple chunks, mango chunks, and kiwi fruit quarters**

New Year's Television-Watching Party

Mexican Green Chile Fondue (page 30)
  Dippers: **Poached shrimp, jicama sticks, and red and gold bell pepper strips**

Tortilla chips

Butterscotch Fondue (page 88)
  Dippers: **Strawberries, banana chunks, pineapple chunks, peach slices, kiwi fruit slices**

Sparkling apple cider and sparkling cranberry juice

EQUIPMENT

There are many styles of fondue pots, and some work better for certain types of fondue than others.

Thick ceramic or earthenware pots work best for cheese and chocolate fondues, which require low to moderate heat. Pots are available in several sizes. Keep in mind that people eat smaller amounts of chocolate fondue, so the smaller pots are best suited for dessert.

Metal fondue pots—copper, stainless steel, and cast iron—work best for both oil- and broth-based fondues, which require high heat. Models that taper inward at the top prevent oil from splashing.

Many cookware stores carry fondue sets containing both a metal pot and a ceramic insert, making the set useful for cheese, dessert, and oil- or broth-based fondues. Some fondue pots have notches in the sides to hold the fondue forks while the dippers cook. Cast-iron pots with a porcelain glaze and pots with a water jacket suit all types of fondues.

Fuel sources include denatured alcohol, solid-fuel burners, and electric elements. Votive candles are also useful simply for keeping a dessert fondue warm.

Electric fondue pots with thermostatic control are ideal for all types of fondues. Use a low setting of around 150°F for dessert fondues; 170°F for cheese fondues; and 350°F to 375°F for oil fondues. For broth fondues, set the thermostat to 350°F until the broth boils, then reduce to 250°F to simmer.

Other suitable cooking vessels include electric woks, deep electric cook pots, and Mongolian hot pots. Each style has its advantages. It is easy to adjust the temperature on electric pots. Fondue pots using canned heat are more portable. Follow the manufacturer's instructions for using the heating source properly and raising or lowering the heat level to suit your cooking needs.

SAFETY GUIDELINES

Consider wise safety practices when setting up a fondue party:

• Make sure electrical cords are placed so they are not in the walkway or anywhere they could accidentally be knocked loose or pulled.

• Protect the table with a large heat-proof surface between the fondue pot and the table. Use a marble slab, a wood plank, ceramic tiles, or a heat-proof platter.

• Do not overfill the fuel container with denatured alcohol, as it will expand and overflow once ignited.

- Fondue forks should have heat-proof handles. Many sets are color coded so each person can keep track of his or her own fork.

- To avoid crowding, plan on no more than six guests for each fondue pot.

TECHNIQUES

Cheese Fondues

Use ceramic pots exclusively for cheese or chocolate, as these containers are not designed to be brought to high temperatures.

A baguette works well for dicing as it supplies ample crust, and each morsel should contain some crust to keep the bread from dropping into the pot. It is smart to cut the bread an hour or two before serving so it dries out slightly and adheres better to the fork. It is important to swirl the bread chunks in a figure-eight motion, as the fondue should be stirred constantly to prevent burning.

Stir a cheese fondue with a wooden spoon or heat-proof spatula, using a figure-eight motion. Once a cheese fondue has achieved a smooth consistency, keep it warm. If it cools it may toughen and become stringy upon reheating. Leftover cheese fondue is difficult to reheat smoothly. You may have the best success with a microwave.

If a cheese fondue becomes too thick, thin it with a little hot liquid from the original recipe. If it is too thin, add additional shredded cheese or stir in 1 to 2 teaspoons cornstarch blended with 2 tablespoons liquid.

If a cheese fondue separates or forms strings, whisk it vigorously to smooth it out again.

You may choose to start a cheese fondue in a double boiler at the stove top and transfer it to a ceramic pot over low heat at the table.

Entrée Fondues

Use metal pots—copper, stainless steel, or cast iron—for oil- or broth-based fondues.

For oil fondues, use pure canola oil or peanut oil, which can be heated to high temperatures without smoking. Follow the manufacturer's instructions on the amount of oil to use in your pot, as this amount will vary with the size and shape of the pot. Fill the pot no more than one-third full of oil. Always heat oil in an uncovered pot and watch it closely until it is ready.

SERVING FONDUE

To serve a fondue meal, set the table so that each guest has a plate, one or two fondue forks, a standard-size fork, napkins, and, for certain entrée fondues, chopsticks and a small basket strainer.

Cheese fondues may serve as an hors d'oeuvre, first course, or entrée, so the number of servings will vary with each style of service. Because diners often consume more food at a fondue party than at a regular meal, the yield amounts given allow for generous portions.

For a party, it is fun to offer both an entrée and a dessert fondue. For a large sit-down party, count on two fondue pots for each course if the guests number eight to twelve. When serving an entrée fondue, it is often nice to offer a salad alongside each place setting to occupy the guests as their dippers cook.

In warm weather, you may choose to set up the fondue on the patio or in the garden for serving a buffet-style meal.

To determine quantities of dippers to serve per person, figure on $\frac{3}{4}$ to 1 cup bread cubes; 6 to 8 ounces meat, chicken, or fish; $\frac{3}{4}$ cup vegetables; and $\frac{3}{4}$ cup fruit or cookies.

Place labels alongside the sauces and dips to simplify serving and avoid confusion.

Offer appropriate beverages for the occasion. Choices range from beer, wine, and kirsch with savory fondues to coffee, tea, and cappuccino with dessert.

ETIQUETTE

Inform guests of fondue etiquette: Do not eat from the fondue fork that will be returned to the pot. Besides, it might give you a nasty burn if you do. (Provide an extra fork for eating.)

If you drop your bread en route to your plate or mouth, custom allows you to kiss your neighbor. Alternatively, you must buy the next round of drinks.

With a cheese fondue, it is best if only one person dips at a time. With an oil fondue, several forks may rest in the pot, but it is best to not have more than six in the pot at once as too many will cool the oil and keep food from searing quickly. The advantage of using an electric fondue pot is that it can quickly regulate the heat as the forks go into the pot.

Be careful not to dislodge your neighbor's meat when removing your fork from the pot.

CHEESE FONDUES

THE CLASSIC SWISS FONDUE MADE WITH GRUYÈRE AND

Emmentaler launched our devotion to this communal dish. This peasant dish has spawned a potpourri of cheese fondues. Wine, beer, cider, and spirits lend distinctive flavor accents to the creamy sauce, as do various herbs and spices. For variety, I have included a recipe for cheese-less Bagna Cauda (page 35) in this section.

Cheese fondues make equally excellent appetizers and entrées. The number of servings each recipe yields varies greatly depending on the occasion and the crowd. An after-ski gathering must satisfy robust appetites, while a more elegant at-home dinner party will incorporate a number of other dishes.

Classic Swiss Cheese Fondue Neuchâteloise

When I visited the ski slopes of Zermatt, this dish was featured in all the mountain-top chalets. However, each of the different cantons in Switzerland has its own traditional variations, such as alternative cheeses, roasted garlic, morel mushrooms, plum schnapps, or cider. A ceramic or stoneware stub-handled dish called a *coquelon* is traditionally used for cooking and serving this classic fondue.

Authentic Swiss Gruyère and Emmentaler make for a truly memorable feast. A splash of kirsch (or kirschwasser), a clear cherry brandy, is added at the end to produce the desired zing.

It is customary to offer guests a small glass of kirsch halfway through the meal. The golden crust that develops on the bottom of the pot is considered a prized finale to the meal.

8 ounces Emmentaler cheese

8 ounces Gruyère cheese

2 tablespoons cornstarch

1 clove garlic, halved

2 cups dry white wine, such as
   Rhine Riesling

3 tablespoons kirsch

Dash of freshly grated nutmeg

Salt and white pepper (optional)

DIPPERS
2 baguettes, cut into bite-sized cubes,
each with some crust on

Shred both cheeses coarsely or dice them into ¼-inch pieces. Toss the shredded cheese lightly with the cornstarch until evenly coated.

Rub the insides of a fondue pot with the garlic and discard the garlic. Pour the wine into the pot and set over low heat until bubbles rise. Gradually add the cheese, a handful at a time, stirring each time until the cheese is completely melted. Avoid letting the mixture come to a boil. Stir in the kirsch. Sprinkle with nutmeg and season to taste with salt and white pepper, if using.

Serve with a basket of crusty bread cubes to dunk into the sauce.

MAKES 4 TO 6 SERVINGS

Scotch Highland Fondue

In the highlands of Scotland, a jigger of Scotch might imbue a winter fondue with a lively fillip. Gild speared cubes of rye, onion, or pumpernickel bread with this zesty cheese fondue. Consider red- and green-skinned apples as another embellishment during the holiday season.

1 tablespoon butter

1 small yellow onion, finely chopped

1¼ cups whole milk

1 pound sharp Cheddar cheese, shredded

1 tablespoon cornstarch

¼ cup Scotch whiskey

DIPPERS
1 loaf country-style rye, onion, or pumpernickel bread, cut into bite-size cubes, each with some crust on; apple slices, and/or pear slices

In a 2-quart saucepan over medium heat, melt the butter and sauté the onion until soft, about 5 minutes. Add the milk and heat until bubbles form. Gradually add the cheese, a handful at a time, stirring each time until the cheese is completely melted. In a small bowl, blend together the cornstarch and whiskey; stir into the cheese mixture and cook until blended, 2 to 3 minutes. Transfer to a fondue pot and keep warm over low heat.

Serve with bowls of bread cubes and sliced apples or pears.

MAKES 4 TO 6 SERVINGS

Lobster Gruyère Fondue

Fresh-cooked lobster lends a luscious richness to this wine-scented fondue. For ease, consider utilizing a 6-ounce tail. You might complete the menu with a field-green salad strewn with sliced cremini mushrooms and diced oil-cured sun-dried tomatoes. Finish off with a basket of fresh seasonal fruit: peaches or nectarines, Bing cherries, apricots, and grapes.

1 pound Gruyère or Jarlsberg cheese

2 tablespoons cornstarch

1¾ cups dry white wine, such as Rhine Riesling

3 tablespoons Pernod

6 ounces cooked lobster meat, finely chopped

Salt and white pepper or cayenne pepper (optional)

DIPPERS
2 sourdough baguettes, cut into bite-size cubes, each with some crust on

Shred the cheese coarsely or dice it into ¼-inch pieces. Toss the shredded cheese lightly with the cornstarch until evenly coated. Pour the wine into a fondue pot and set over low heat until bubbles rise. Gradually add the cheese, a handful at a time, stirring each time until the cheese is completely melted. Avoid letting the mixture come to a boil. Stir in the Pernod and lobster meat. Sprinkle with salt and white pepper or cayenne pepper, if using.

Serve with a basket of crusty bread cubes to dunk into the sauce.

MAKES 4 TO 6 SERVINGS

Jarlsberg-Crab Fondue

Your guests will return their forks over and over to this delectable fresh crab fondue, relishing every bite. It works best to dry the sourdough bread cubes slightly so the coating clings to them nicely. Serve with a bountiful salad of field greens, avocado slices, and pink grapefruit segments or red and gold cherry tomatoes. Follow the fondue with a lemon tart or a dessert fondue.

8 ounces Jarlsberg cheese

8 ounces Gruyère cheese

2 tablespoons cornstarch

2 cups dry white wine, such as
 Rhine Riesling

3 tablespoons dry sherry

1½ cups fresh crabmeat, shredded
 and picked over for shells

Dash of freshly grated nutmeg

Salt and white pepper (optional)

DIPPERS
2 sourdough baguettes, cut into bite-
size cubes, each with some crust on

Shred both cheeses coarsely or dice them into ¼-inch pieces. Toss the shredded cheese lightly with the cornstarch until evenly coated.

Pour the wine into a fondue pot and set over low heat until bubbles rise. Gradually add the cheese, a handful at a time, stirring each time until the cheese is completely melted. Avoid letting the mixture come to a boil. Stir in the sherry and crabmeat. Sprinkle with nutmeg and season to taste with salt and white pepper, if using.

Serve with a basket of crusty bread cubes to dunk into the sauce.

MAKES 4 TO 6 SERVINGS

Bavarian Beer Fondue

This hearty dish can make a full meal or stand in for an appetizer. It is fun to offer a colorful array of potatoes to dip: yellow Yukon Golds, red-skinned Blisses, and Peruvian purple potatoes. Instead of chicken-apple sausages, you can serve tiny frankfurters, cooked and sliced bratwurst, or wine-and-cheese sausages. Round out the menu with a warm fruit tart or apple strudel. A full-bodied red or dark beer will enhance the flavor of this fondue.

1½ cups beer or dark ale

2 cloves garlic, minced

8 ounces mild Cheddar cheese, shredded

8 ounces sharp Cheddar cheese, shredded

2 tablespoons cornstarch

1 teaspoon whole-grain or Dijon mustard

DIPPERS
2 sourdough baguettes, cut into bite-size cubes, each with some crust on; apple slices; sliced cooked chicken-apple sausages; and/or cooked Yukon Gold, Red Bliss, or purple potatoes, halved or quartered

Small cornichons or dill pickles for serving

In a fondue pot over medium heat, heat the beer with the garlic until bubbles appear. Toss the cheese lightly with the cornstarch until evenly coated and add a handful at a time, stirring each time until the cheese is completely melted. Stir in the mustard and keep warm over low heat.

Serve with the sourdough bread cubes, apple slices, sausages, and/or potatoes. Offer cornichons on the side.

MAKES 4 TO 6 SERVINGS

Norman Cheese and Apple Fondue

Apples—in the form of cider and Calvados—lend a double fruitiness to this fondue, which is slightly sweet. Lemon juice counters with a welcome piquancy. This recipe, based on the cuisine of Normandy, is delightful with crisp apple slices, Anjou or red-skinned Bartlett pears, and crusty sourdough French bread. Consider following the fondue with a light entrée such as trout amandine with chive-coated new potatoes.

1¼ cups apple cider

1½ tablespoons freshly squeezed lemon juice

12 ounces (3 cups) shredded French Comté, Gruyère, or Swiss cheese

2 tablespoons cornstarch

12 tablespoons Calvados or Cognac

2 teaspoons Dijon mustard

Salt and freshly ground black pepper

DIPPERS
Apple slices; pear slices; and/or 2 sourdough baguettes, cut into bite-size cubes, each with some crust on

In a fondue pot over medium heat, heat the cider and lemon juice until bubbles form. Toss the cheese lightly with the cornstarch until evenly coated, then gradually add to the pot, a handful at a time, stirring each time until the cheese is completely melted. Stir in the Calvados, mustard, and salt and pepper to taste. Keep warm over low heat.

Serve with sliced apples, sliced pears, and crusty bread cubes for dipping.

MAKES 4 TO 6 SERVINGS

Fonduta

In Tuscany, during the autumn truffle season, fonduta is a renowned antipasto course. With fresh truffles costing as much as they do, feel free to add a few drops of a good-quality white truffle oil or paste right before you serve the fonduta so its pungency will not fade. A favorite pasta dish and Caesar salad would make fine accompaniments.

1¼ cups dry white wine, such as Pinot Grigio, or sparkling wine

12 ounces (3 cups) shredded fontina cheese

1 tablespoon cornstarch

2 large egg yolks

Salt and white pepper (optional)

Few drops truffle oil, 1 teaspoon truffle paste, or finely chopped truffles (see note)

DIPPERS
2 sweet (not sourdough) baguettes, cut into bite-size cubes, each with some crust on; small mushrooms, trimmed and halved; and/or cooked artichoke hearts, halved

In the top of a double boiler set over simmering water, heat 1 cup of the wine until steaming. Toss the cheese lightly with the cornstarch until evenly coated. Gradually add the cheese to the pot, a handful at a time, stirring each time until the cheese is completely melted. In a small bowl, whisk the egg yolks together with the remaining ¼ cup wine. Pour the egg mixture into the cheese mixture and cook until thickened, stirring constantly. Season with salt and white pepper to taste, if using. Just before serving, stir in the truffle oil. Transfer to a fondue pot and keep warm over low heat, or serve in preheated individual ramekins.

Pass the bread cubes, mushrooms, and artichoke hearts for dipping.

MAKES 4 TO 6 SERVINGS

Note:
Minced truffles are quite expensive, so you may want to budget for a small amount as a special treat for this recipe. Otherwise, truffle oil or truffle paste will work nicely.

Dutch Caramelized Onion–Smoked Gouda Fondue

The caramel sweetness of long-sautéed onion adds an intriguing accent to this creamy, smoky fondue. Consider serving this fondue accompanied by a salad of Belgian endives and toasted walnuts, with small Yukon Gold potatoes tossed in parsley butter on the side and a dessert of warm baked apples or wine-steeped Bosc pears and whipped cream.

1 tablespoon olive oil

1 tablespoon butter

1 large yellow onion, coarsely chopped

2 teaspoons sugar

2 cups dry white wine, such as Rhine Riesling

8 ounces smoked Gouda cheese, shredded

8 ounces Emmentaler, Gruyère, or Swiss cheese, shredded

2 tablespoons cornstarch

Salt and freshly ground black pepper

DIPPERS
Crusty dark bread or rye bread, cut into bite-size cubes, each with some crust on; red and gold cherry or plum tomatoes; and/or fennel bulbs, cut diagonally into 1-inch chunks

In a medium skillet over medium-high heat, heat the olive oil and butter. Add the onion and sauté for 5 minutes, stirring often. Reduce the heat to low, sprinkle the onion with the sugar, and cook, stirring until the onion is melted down and light brown, about 15 minutes longer. In a fondue pot over medium heat, heat the wine until bubbles form. Add the onion. Toss the cheeses lightly with the cornstarch until evenly coated. Gradually add the cheeses to the pot, a handful at a time, stirring each time until the cheeses are completely melted. Season with salt and pepper to taste and keep warm over low heat.

Serve with crusty bread cubes, tomatoes, and fennel for dipping.

MAKES 4 TO 6 SERVINGS

Tuscan Cheese Fondue

Two renowned Italian cheeses intermingle in this zesty cheese fondue, which is perfect for dipping mushrooms, artichokes, and bread sticks in. Swirling basil pesto into the sauce, as the variation suggests, gives it an aromatic herb overtone that enhances vegetable dippers.

1½ cups dry white wine, such as Pinot Grigio

2 large cloves garlic, minced

12 ounces (3 cups) shredded fontina cheese

4 ounces (1 cup) shredded Asiago or Parmesan cheese

2 tablespoons cornstarch

DIPPERS
Brown cremini mushrooms, trimmed and halved; small cooked artichoke hearts, halved; red or gold cherry tomatoes; and/or bread sticks, broken into bite-size pieces

In a fondue pot over medium heat, heat the wine and garlic until bubbles form. Toss the cheeses lightly with the cornstarch until evenly coated. Gradually add the cheeses to the pot, a handful at a time, stirring each time until the cheeses are completely melted.

Serve with bowls of the vegetables and bread sticks to dip into the sauce.

MAKES 4 TO 6 SERVINGS

Variation:
Tuscan Cheese Pesto Fondue: Prepare the Tuscan Cheese Fondue as directed above, then stir in 2 to 3 tablespoons Basil Pesto (page 73) or a commercial pesto just before serving.

Mexican Green Chile Fondue

This rich but zingy cheese dip calls out for shrimp, crunchy vegetables, or apples. It is well suited for an informal backyard party or for sports fans gathered around the television. Offer a basket of spicy tortilla chips alongside for munching and dipping.

1½ cups whole milk

8 ounces Monterey Jack cheese, shredded

8 ounces sharp Cheddar cheese, shredded

2 tablespoons cornstarch

½ teaspoon ground coriander

½ teaspoon ground cumin

One 4-ounce can diced green chiles, drained

Dash of liquid hot pepper seasoning (optional)

DIPPERS
Cooked medium shrimp, peeled and deveined; jicama sticks; red and gold bell pepper strips; zucchini slices; and/or apple slices

Tortilla chips for serving

In a fondue pot over medium heat, heat the milk until bubbles form. Toss the cheeses lightly with cornstarch until evenly coated. Gradually add the cheeses to the pot, a handful at a time, stirring each time until the cheeses are completely melted. Stir in the coriander, cumin, chiles, and hot pepper seasoning, if using, and keep warm over low heat.

Serve with shrimp, vegetables, and apples for dipping. Pass a basket of tortilla chips.

MAKES 4 TO 6 SERVINGS

Queso Fundido

Queso fundido (Spanish for "melted cheese") is Mexico's take on fondue—the creamy sauce is spiked with hot salsa. This classic recipe dates back a few decades to my early days styling food and writing for *Sunset* magazine. Red and green bell pepper strips make a colorful, crunchy dipper, or try the cool-tasting jicama.

1 tablespoon olive oil

1 medium yellow onion, chopped

1 clove garlic, minced

One 15-ounce can diced tomatoes, drained

One 4-ounce can chopped green chiles, drained

8 ounces Monterey Jack cheese, shredded

8 ounces mild Cheddar cheese, shredded

½ cup unflavored yogurt or buttermilk

Dash of hot pepper sauce

DIPPERS
Tortilla chips, red and green bell pepper strips, jicama sticks, and celery sticks

In a 2-quart saucepan over medium heat, heat the oil and sauté the onion until soft. Add the garlic, tomatoes, and chiles and cook for 5 minutes. Remove from the heat and gradually add the cheeses a handful at a time, stirring each time until the cheeses are completely melted. Stir in the yogurt and hot pepper sauce. Transfer to a fondue pot and keep warm over low heat.

Serve with tortilla chips, bell pepper strips, jicama sticks, and celery sticks to dip into the sauce.

MAKES 6 TO 8 SERVINGS

Welsh Rarebit

Sometimes called "Welsh Rabbit," this old-time family dish was often served poured over whole-grain toast. Try serving it instead as a fondue that your family can dip assorted vegetables into. Traditionally, the cheese should be a sharp Cheddar and the liquid a dark ale, but for family dining you may choose to substitute a milder Cheddar for the sharp cheese and apple juice or milk for the beer and sherry. Broiled hamburgers or turkey burgers, coleslaw, and chocolate chip cookies would round out a family meal.

2 tablespoons all-purpose flour

2 teaspoons dry mustard

2 tablespoons butter

½ cup whole milk

1 cup dark ale

1 pound sharp Cheddar cheese, diced

¼ cup dry sherry or apple juice

Salt and freshly ground black pepper

DIPPERS
Red and yellow cherry tomatoes, green and yellow zucchini sticks, celery sticks, carrot slices, apple wedges, broccoli florets (blanched for one minute in boiling water, if preferred), and/or sesame bread sticks

In a medium saucepan over medium heat, stir together the flour, mustard, and butter until blended. Gradually stir in the milk and ale. Heat slowly, stirring constantly until the sauce boils and thickens. Reduce the heat to low and gradually add the cheese, a handful at a time, stirring each time until the cheese is completely melted. Stir in the sherry until blended and season with salt and pepper to taste. Transfer to a fondue pot and keep warm over low heat.

   Serve with raw vegetables, apple wedges, and bread sticks for dipping into the sauce.

MAKES 4 TO 6 SERVINGS

Bagna Cauda

The name of this Italian classic means "hot bath." It invites a wide assortment of both raw and blanched vegetables for dipping. You can use good-quality canned anchovies or purchase loose-pack anchovies from a specialty market. Because this dish is rather messy to serve, it is ideal for an outdoor garden party. Just set up the fondue pot on a patio table.

Some of my friends who were of Italian heritage used to stage an annual party around this dish. Guests would bring either vegetables for dipping or a dessert. Custom decreed that eating bagna cauda would bring good health throughout the year.

½ cup olive oil

½ cup (1 stick) butter

4 cloves garlic, finely chopped

6 anchovies (canned or
loose-pack), diced

Pinch of red pepper flakes (optional)

Salt and freshly ground
black pepper

DIPPERS
Red and gold bell pepper strips; celery or fennel strips; carrot slices or baby carrots; small mushroom caps; red or gold cherry tomatoes; zucchini or yellow summer squash slices; jicama slices; snow peas, ends trimmed and blanched for 1 minute in boiling water; cauliflower florets, blanched for 1 minute in boiling water; broccoli florets, blanched for 1 minute in boiling water; cooked whole artichokes; and/or sourdough bread, thinly sliced

In a fondue pot over medium-low heat, combine the olive oil, butter, garlic, anchovies, and red pepper flakes, if using. Season with salt and pepper to taste. Heat until the butter is melted, stirring to blend all ingredients. Reduce the heat to low; the mixture should stay warm but the butter should not brown.

Arrange your choice of 5 to 6 vegetable dippers on a platter at the table or in individual salad bowls. Guests can dip a vegetable into the bagna cauda and use a slice of bread to catch the drips.

MAKES 6 TO 8 APPETIZER SERVINGS

Oregon Fruit Harvest Buttermilk Fondue

Growing up in Oregon's verdant Willamette Valley, I enjoyed this tangy fondue as a Sunday night supper. We would dip in fruit we picked from the backyard orchard—Jonathan apples and Bartlett pears—plus Mother's homemade toasted hazelnut or three-grain bread. We always made the fondue with sharp Cheddar that we would slice off a big block of the cheese in the basement fruit room. Every month Daddy, a wholesale grocer, would drive his green pickup truck to the coast to pick up wheels of Tillamook Cheddar from the local creamery.

2 cups buttermilk

1 pound sharp Cheddar cheese, shredded

3 tablespoons cornstarch

½ teaspoon salt

¼ teaspoon white pepper

Dash of freshly grated nutmeg

DIPPERS
Apple slices; pear slices; and/or
1 loaf walnut-raisin bread or
2 baguettes, cut into bite-size
cubes, each with some crust on

In the top of a double boiler over simmering water or in a 2-quart saucepan over medium heat, heat the buttermilk until bubbles form. (Don't worry if the mixture looks curdled, as it will smooth out.) Toss the cheese lightly with the cornstarch, salt, pepper, and nutmeg until evenly coated. Gradually add the cheese to the buttermilk mixture, a handful at a time, stirring each time until the cheese is completely melted. Transfer to a fondue pot and keep warm over low heat.

Serve with sliced apples, sliced pears, and cubed walnut-raisin bread or baguette for dipping into the sauce.

MAKES 4 TO 6 SERVINGS

ENTRÉE FONDUES

WHAT FUN IT IS FOR FAMILY AND FRIENDS TO SHARE A

meal they cook together! Here a wide choice of entrées—including beef, lamb, pork, chicken, duck, and seafood—offers lots of options for dinners and parties. The cooking mediums vary from oil to broth to please all tastes. The best part of serving entrée fondues is that preparations are easily done in advance so you, the host, can be a guest at the party, too.

Plan to serve at least two sauces—and, ideally, three or four—with an entrée fondue. Place the sauces within easy reach of all the guests, or pass them on a tray for a large dinner. Serve very runny sauces in individual tiny bowls.

Filet Mignon and Shrimp Fondue

For Christmas Eve dinner, it is a holiday tradition for many families to serve this special entrée around the communal table. In the San Francisco Bay Area, my friend Claire Stewart Kostic sets a stunning table for a dozen, with two fondue pots on ceramic tiles spaced on the embroidered cloth her grandmother purchased in China in the 1930s. Red tapers, red roses, a gilt centerpiece sleigh, and party favors add décor. The menu (see page 10) enchants all ages. Her sister Sandy Stevenson in New Caanan, Connecticut, also sets forth two fondue pots on this holiday eve—one for meat eaters and one exclusively for vegetarians.

Most of the sauces listed below work beautifully with either meat, and their flavors will please both adults and children.

MARINADE

3 tablespoons freshly squeezed
  lemon juice

2 tablespoons olive oil

2 cloves garlic, minced

1 green onion (white part only),
  finely chopped

¼ teaspoon fines herbes or herbs
  of Provence

1 pound filet mignon or other beef
  steak, such as sirloin or tenderloin,
  cut into 1-inch pieces

Canola or peanut oil for the fondue pot

1 pound medium raw shrimp, peeled
  and deveined

SUGGESTED SAUCES
Basil Pesto (page 73), Horseradish–
Sour Cream Sauce (page 65),
Sour Cream–Dill Sauce (page 67),
Chile-Peanut Sauce (page 72), and/or
Tomato Cocktail Sauce (page 67)

To prepare the marinade: In a small bowl, stir together the lemon juice, olive oil, garlic, green onion, and herbs. Put the beef into a resealable bag, pour in the marinade, and marinate, sealed, in the refrigerator for 1 to 2 hours. Bring to room temperature before cooking.

Fill a metal fondue pot one-third full with oil and heat the oil to 375°F, or until a cube of bread browns in 30 seconds. Drain the meat, pat dry, and set out with the shrimp and 2 to 4 of the sauces. With fondue forks or heat-proof chopsticks, cook the meat until medium-rare, about 2 minutes, and cook the shrimp until it turns pink, 1 to 2 minutes. Dip into the sauces.

MAKES 4 TO 6 SERVINGS

Beef Bourguignonne Fondue

Marinating the steak promotes its tenderness and imbues the meat with considerable flavor. To enhance the richness of the fondue, replace ½ cup of the cooking oil with one stick of unsalted butter.

MARINADE
¼ cup dry red wine, such as Pinot Noir

1 tablespoon olive oil

1 teaspoon Dijon mustard

2 cloves garlic, minced

1 green onion (white part only),
   finely chopped

2 pounds boneless beef, such as sirloin
   or tenderloin, cut into 1-inch pieces

Canola or peanut oil for the fondue pot

SUGGESTED SAUCES
Béarnaise Sauce (page 66),
Horseradish–Sour Cream Sauce
(page 65), and/or Sun-Dried
Tomato–Balsamic Sauce (page 74)

To prepare the marinade: In a medium bowl, stir together the wine, olive oil, mustard, garlic, and green onion. Put the beef into a resealable bag, pour in the marinade, and marinate, sealed, in the refrigerator for 1 to 2 hours. Bring to room temperature before cooking.

Fill a metal fondue pot one-third full with oil and heat the oil to 375°F, or until a cube of bread browns in 30 seconds. Drain the meat, pat dry, and set out with the sauces. With fondue forks or heat-proof chopsticks, cook the meat until medium-rare, about 2 minutes. Dip into the sauces.

MAKES 4 TO 6 SERVINGS

Beef Teriyaki Fondue

This classic Japanese marinade is excellent with choice steak, such as sirloin or top loin, and served with a bowl of hot rice and quickly sautéed snow peas on the side. You might accompany the meal with a watercress, endive, and tangerine salad and end with mango or lime sorbet.

MARINADE
⅓ cup sake or dry sherry

⅓ cup soy sauce

2 tablespoons sugar

2 teaspoons grated peeled
  fresh ginger

1 clove garlic, minced

½ teaspoon Asian-style sesame oil

2 slices lemon

2 pounds lean beef sirloin or top loin,
  cut into 1½-by-½-inch strips

Canola or peanut oil for the fondue pot

SUGGESTED SAUCES
Chile-Peanut Sauce (page 72),
Ponzu (page 72), Sesame-
Cilantro Sauce (page 70), and/or
Soy-Wasabi Sauce (page 70)

To prepare the marinade: In a medium bowl, stir together the sake, soy sauce, sugar, ginger, garlic, sesame oil, and lemon. Put the beef into a resealable bag, pour in the marinade, and marinate, sealed, for 1 hour at room temperature or up to 3 hours in the refrigerator. Bring to room temperature before cooking.

Fill a metal fondue pot one-third full with oil and heat the oil to 375°F, or until a cube of bread browns in 30 seconds. Drain the meat, pat dry, and set out with the sauces. With fondue forks or heat-proof chopsticks, cook the meat until it is medium-rare, about 2 minutes. Dip into the sauces.

MAKES 4 TO 6 SERVINGS

Greek Island Lamb Fondue

Lamb traditionally is the centerpiece of our Paschal menu, and this lamb fondue makes an appealing change of pace for Easter Sunday dinner, creating an intimate holiday atmosphere. A spinach salad sparked with strawberries, a pilaf, and steamed asparagus with shaved Kasseri cheese would make appealing accompaniments. End the meal with almond soufflé cake and honey-Cointreau ice cream.

MARINADE
¼ cup dry red wine, such as Pinot Noir

1 tablespoon canola oil

2 cloves garlic, minced

1 teaspoon minced fresh
  rosemary sprigs

1 teaspoon salt

¼ teaspoon freshly ground
  black pepper

2 pounds boneless leg of lamb,
  cut into 1-inch pieces

Canola or peanut oil for the fondue pot

SUGGESTED SAUCES
Aioli (page 68),
Yogurt Sauce with Mint (page 75),
and/or Sun-Dried Tomato–Balsamic
Sauce (page 74)

To prepare the marinade: In a medium bowl, stir together the wine, oil, garlic, rosemary, salt, and pepper. Put the lamb into a resealable bag, pour in the marinade, and marinate, sealed, in the refrigerator for 1 to 2 hours. Bring to room temperature before cooking.

Fill a metal fondue pot one-third full with oil and heat the oil to 375°F, or until a cube of bread browns in 30 seconds. Drain the meat, pat dry, and set out with the sauces. With fondue forks or heat-proof chopsticks, cook the meat until medium-rare, about 2 minutes. Dip into the sauces.

MAKES 4 TO 6 SERVINGS

Lamb Curry Fondue

Lively condiments enhance these spicy lamb bites. To round out the meal and cool tingling palates, you might serve each guest a bowl of steamed rice and skewers of colorful melon balls.

MARINADE
3 tablespoons freshly squeezed
  lime juice

3 tablespoons canola oil

2 cloves garlic, minced

2 green onions (white part only),
  minced

2 teaspoons curry powder

1 teaspoon minced peeled
  fresh ginger

½ teaspoon salt

¼ teaspoon freshly ground
  black pepper

2 pounds boneless leg of lamb,
  cut into 1-inch pieces

Canola or peanut oil for the fondue pot

SUGGESTED SAUCES
Chutney-Curry Sauce (page 65),
Chile-Peanut Sauce (page 72),
Yogurt Sauce with Cilantro (page 75),
and/or Sesame-Cilantro Sauce
(page 70)

To prepare the marinade: In a small bowl, stir together the lime juice, oil, garlic, green onions, curry powder, ginger, salt, and pepper. Put the lamb into a resealable bag, pour in the marinade, and marinate, sealed, in the refrigerator for 1 to 2 hours. Bring to room temperature before cooking.

Fill a metal fondue pot one-third full with oil and heat the oil to 375°F, or until a cube of bread browns in 30 seconds. Drain the meat, pat dry, and set out with the sauces. With fondue forks or heat-proof chopsticks, cook the meat until medium-rare, about 2 minutes. Dip into the sauces.

MAKES 4 TO 6 SERVINGS

Shabu-Shabu

The name of this Japanese dish, *shabu-shabu,* describes the swishing sound that you make with your chopsticks when you swirl morsels of meat around in the simmering broth. The meat cooks swiftly, while the vegetables take a little longer. Once everything is cooked, ladle the broth into small bowls or cups for sipping.

In Japan, Shabu-Shabu is made in an earthenware casserole called a *donabe* or in a Mongolian hot pot, or *hoko-nabe.* You can achieve fine results using an electric wok or an electric fondue pot. Very cold or partially frozen meat is easier to slice thinly.

2 pounds well-marbled sirloin or prime beef, sliced paper thin

12 fresh shiitake mushrooms, wiped and trimmed, halved if large

8 green onions (including tops), cut diagonally into 1½-inch lengths

½ small Chinese (napa) cabbage, cut into 2-inch pieces

12 small spinach leaves

1 pound firm tofu, cut into 1¼-inch cubes

6 ounces udon noodles, cooked and drained (optional)

½ cup finely chopped green onions (including tops)

6 to 8 cups beef broth

SUGGESTED SAUCES
Sesame-Cilantro Sauce (page 70), Ponzu (page 72), and/or Soy-Wasabi Sauce (page 70)

Arrange the beef, mushrooms, green onion pieces, cabbage, spinach, tofu, noodles, if using, and chopped green onions on a platter at the table, and set out the sauces in small bowls. Fill an electric wok or fondue pot two-thirds full of the broth. Bring the broth to a boil, reduce the heat, and simmer gently for 2 minutes.

Provide each diner with chopsticks or a fondue fork. Cook the mushrooms, green onion pieces, and cabbage in the broth for 1 to 2 minutes, then add the meat, spinach, and tofu and cook 2 more minutes. Diners may choose to add one-fourth of the meat and vegetables at a time and then dip the cooked morsels into the sauces provided. When all the diners have had their fill of the vegetables and meat, add the noodles, if using, to the broth and heat through. Finally, add the chopped green onions to the broth and ladle into small bowls for sipping.

MAKES 4 TO 6 SERVINGS

Asian Duck and Vegetables in Broth

My friends Cathy and Don Priest make this dish with wild goose. (Wild duck would be too strong in flavor and too low in fat.)

MARINADE
¼ cup soy sauce

2 teaspoons brown sugar

1 teaspoon Asian-style sesame oil

1 teaspoon crushed coriander seeds
  or ground coriander

1½ pounds boneless, skinless duck
  breasts, thinly sliced

1 large yam, peeled, quartered,
  and cut into ¼-inch-thick slices

3 medium carrots, thinly sliced

12 ounces broccoli florets

12 small fresh shiitake or brown
  cremini mushrooms, trimmed

1 medium yellow onion, halved, and
  thinly sliced

4 Chinese (napa) cabbage leaves,
  cut into 2-inch pieces

5 to 6 cups chicken broth

½-inch piece fresh ginger, peeled and
  thinly sliced

CONDIMENTS AND
SUGGESTED SAUCES
Chopped green onions (tops included);
soy sauce; chile oil; hoisin sauce;
Chile-Peanut Sauce (page 72); Teriyaki
Sauce (page 74); and
Soy-Wasabi Sauce (page 70)

To prepare the marinade: In a medium bowl, stir together the soy sauce, brown sugar, sesame oil, and coriander. Add the duck and let marinate at room temperature for 1 hour.

Arrange the duck, yam, carrots, broccoli, mushrooms, onion, and cabbage on a platter at the table. Provide each diner with a soup bowl, a pair of chopsticks, and a perforated ladle for lifting cooked morsels out of the broth. Fill an electric wok or fondue pot two-thirds full of the broth. Bring the broth to a boil with the ginger, reduce the heat, and simmer gently for 3 to 4 minutes.

Cook the ingredients in two or three batches as follows: Cook the yam, carrots, and broccoli first for 4 to 5 minutes. Then add the mushrooms, onion, and cabbage and cook for another 1 to 2 minutes. Finally, add the duck, cover the pot and bring to a boil, and cook for about 2 minutes. Ladle the cooked duck and vegetables into the bowls with a little broth and season with the condiments and sauces. When all the diners have had their fill of the vegetables and duck, ladle the remaining broth into the bowls for sipping.

MAKES 4 TO 6 SERVINGS

Chinese Steamboat

My friend Tong Sun says, "Mama used to call us with 'Hurry, hurry, come have Chinese Steamboat!'" She is of Hakka heritage, but grew up in Malaysia. As a child, her family would sit around the table, dipping their chopsticks into a pot of meat and vegetables and savoring it all before slurping the broth. Now Tong Sun carries on this tradition with her California family and friends. But instead of the traditional Chinese "steamboat" cooking vessel, she sets an electric wok on the table; a deep electric fondue pot would also work well.

1½ pounds boneless, skinless chicken breasts, pork loin, and/or beef, thinly sliced

Salt and freshly ground black pepper

1 tablespoon grated peeled fresh ginger

2 cloves garlic, chopped

1 tablespoon plus 1 teaspoon Asian-style sesame oil, divided

12 fresh small brown cremini or shiitake mushrooms, trimmed and halved if large

8 green onions (including tops), cut diagonally into 1½-inch lengths

2 celery stalks, cut diagonally into ¼-inch-thick slices

2 medium carrots, cut diagonally into ¼-inch-thick slices

8 ounces asparagus, cut diagonally into 1½-inch lengths (optional)

1 pound firm tofu, cut into 1-inch cubes

1 bunch bok choy, cut into 2-inch lengths

16 small spinach leaves

4 ounces snow peas, ends trimmed

8 ounces cellophane noodles, softened in hot water for 10 minutes and drained

5 to 6 cups chicken broth

½-inch piece fresh ginger, thinly sliced

CONDIMENTS AND SUGGESTED SAUCES
Finely chopped garlic, minced peeled fresh ginger, thinly sliced jalapeño peppers, chopped green onion (including tops), soy sauce, chile oil, Sesame-Cilantro Sauce (page 70), and/or Chile-Peanut Sauce (page 72)

Season the meats with salt and pepper. In a medium bowl, stir together the grated ginger, garlic, and 1 tablespoon of the sesame oil. Add the meats and toss to coat evenly and let marinate at room temperature for 45 minutes to 1 hour.

Arrange the meats, mushrooms, green onion pieces, celery, carrots, asparagus, if using, tofu, bok choy, spinach, snow peas, and noodles on a platter at the table.

(continued)

Provide each diner with a soup bowl, a pair of chopsticks, and a perforated ladle for lifting cooked morsels out of the broth. Fill an electric wok or fondue pot two-thirds full of the broth. Bring the broth to a boil, with the ginger slices and the remaining 1 teaspoon sesame oil, reduce the heat, and simmer gently for 3 to 4 minutes.

Cook the ingredients in two or three batches as follows: Cook the mushrooms, green onion pieces, celery, carrots, and asparagus (if using) first for 2 minutes. Then add the meats and tofu, and finally the bok choy, spinach, and snow peas. Cover and bring to a boil and cook for 2 minutes. Ladle the cooked meats and vegetables into the bowls with a little broth and season with the condiments and sauces. When all the diners have had their fill of the vegetables and meats, add the noodles to the broth and heat through. Ladle the noodles and broth into the bowls for sipping.

MAKES 4 TO 6 SERVINGS

Note:
To make the noodles easier to serve and eat, cut them into 4-inch lengths before adding them to the broth.

Variation:
Vegetarian Steamboat: Omit the chicken, pork, and/or beef. Substitute a good-quality vegetable broth for the chicken broth and increase the amount of tofu to 2 pounds, marinating it in Teriyaki Sauce (page 74) for 1 hour before cooking. Cook as directed above.

Hawaiian Pork Fondue

Three assertive Asian seasonings—soy, ginger, and sesame oil—impart a rich flavor to skewered chunks of pork. Vibrant sauces put it over the top. A fun accent for this entrée would be skewers of fresh pineapple chunks striped with red bell pepper wedges.

MARINADE
3 tablespoons soy sauce

1½ tablespoons red wine vinegar

1 tablespoon canola oil

1 tablespoon honey or brown sugar

2 cloves garlic, minced

½ teaspoon Asian-style sesame oil

2 teaspoons minced peeled fresh ginger

2 pounds boneless pork tenderloin
   or loin, cut into 1-inch pieces

Canola or peanut oil for the fondue pot

SUGGESTED SAUCES
Chile-Peanut Sauce (page 72),
Chutney-Curry Sauce (page 65),
Yogurt Sauce with Oregano (page 75),
and/or commercially prepared
sweet-hot mustard

To prepare the marinade: In a small bowl, stir together the soy sauce, vinegar, oil, honey, garlic, sesame oil, and ginger. Put the pork into a resealable bag, pour in the marinade, and let stand, sealed, at room temperature for 1 hour.

Fill a metal fondue pot one-third full with oil and heat the oil to 375°F, or until a cube of bread browns in 30 seconds. Drain the meat, pat dry, and set out with the sauces. With fondue forks or heat-proof chopsticks, cook the meat until no longer pink inside, 2 to 3 minutes. Dip into the sauces.

MAKES 4 TO 6 SERVINGS

Indonesian Turkey or Pork Saté

Lively Southeast Asian saté seasonings have been a favorite of mine for broiled meat kebabs. Searing the spiced meat in hot oil will achieve much the same effect as broiling. Accompany the saté with couscous or brown rice, skewers of fresh pineapple and red bell peppers, and blanched asparagus or broccoli. For dessert, serve the Candied Ginger, Lemon, and Cream Cheese Fondue (page 91).

MARINADE

1 medium yellow onion, chopped

2 teaspoons freshly ground coriander seeds or ¾ teaspoon ground coriander

Dash of cayenne pepper

1½ tablespoons packed brown sugar

2 cloves garlic, minced

3 tablespoons freshly squeezed lemon juice

1 teaspoon curry powder

3 tablespoons soy sauce

1 tablespoon canola or peanut oil

½ teaspoon salt

¼ teaspoon freshly ground black pepper

2 pounds boneless, skinless turkey breasts or lean pork cubes, cut into 1-inch chunks

Canola or peanut oil for the fondue pot

SUGGESTED SAUCES
Chutney-Curry Sauce (page 65), Sesame-Cilantro Sauce (page 70), and/or Chile-Peanut Sauce (page 72)

To prepare the marinade: In a small bowl, stir together the onion, coriander, cayenne pepper, brown sugar, garlic, lemon juice, curry powder, soy sauce, oil, salt, and black pepper. Put the turkey into a large resealable bag, pour in the marinade, and marinate, sealed, in the refrigerator for 2 to 3 hours. Bring to room temperature before cooking.

Fill a metal fondue pot one-third full with oil and heat the oil to 375°F, or until a cube of bread browns in 30 seconds. Drain the meat, pat dry, and set out with the sauces. With fondue forks or heat-proof chopsticks, cook the meat until no longer pink inside, about 2 minutes. Dip into the sauces.

MAKES 4 TO 6 SERVINGS

Beach Lover's Fish Pot

This is a neat idea for a beach supper set in an informal atmosphere or on an outdoor picnic table. If red snapper is not available, simply ask your fishmonger for the freshest catch of the day. For a richer broth, replace 2 cups of the water with bottled clam juice. In the summertime, you might enjoy sliced heirloom tomatoes and corn on the cob on the side.

Sea salt

16 medium raw shrimp, peeled and deveined

1 pound boneless, skinless red snapper or rockfish fillets, cut into 1-inch pieces

16 mussels or clams in their shells, rinsed under cold water

Lemon wedges for garnish

4 cups water

1 cup dry white wine, such as Sauvignon Blanc

2 tablespoons minced fresh cilantro

SUGGESTED SAUCES
Aioli (page 68), Rémoulade Sauce (page 68), Sesame-Cilantro Sauce (page 70), and/or Tomato Cocktail Sauce (page 67)

Lightly salt the shrimp and red snapper and arrange on a platter at the table with the mussels and lemon wedges. In a fondue pot, bring the water, wine, and cilantro to a boil, then reduce the heat to a gentle simmer. Season with salt to taste. Provide each diner with a soup bowl.

Add the mussels, a few pieces at a time. Cook about 4 minutes. Add the shrimp and red snapper, a few pieces at a time, without crowding the broth, and cook until just opaque and the mussels open, about 2 minutes. Discard any mussels that don't open.

Diners transfer portions to their individual bowls and add a spoonful of one of the sauces and a squeeze of lemon.

MAKES 4 TO 6 SERVINGS

Variation:
Omit shellfish and substitute fishballs or shrimp balls.

Scallop, Shrimp, and Fish Fondue

This fondue makes a beautiful presentation for New Year's Eve or any gala occasion. To complete the festive menu, consider a salad of endive and field greens with pink grapefruit, avocado, and pomegranate seeds, and Caramel-Pecan Fondue (page 86) for dessert.

Sea salt

8 ounces boneless, skinless salmon fillets, cut into 1-inch cubes

8 ounces boneless, skinless halibut or monkfish fillets, cut into 1-inch cubes

6 ounces sea scallops

8 ounces medium-to-large raw shrimp, peeled and deveined

Lemon wedges and cilantro sprigs for garnish

1 tablespoon olive oil

2 shallots, finely chopped

2 cloves garlic, minced

2 teaspoons grated peeled fresh ginger

1 cup dry white wine, such as Sauvignon Blanc

4 cups water

1 teaspoon sea salt

SUGGESTED SAUCES
Sour Cream–Dill Sauce (page 67), Aioli (page 68), Rémoulade Sauce (page 68), Soy-Wasabi Sauce (page 70), Thousand Island Sauce (page 75), and/or Tomato Cocktail Sauce (page 67)

Lightly salt the seafood and chill in the refrigerator until ready to cook. Arrange the seafood on a platter and garnish with the lemon wedges and cilantro sprigs.

In a medium saucepan over medium heat, heat the olive oil and sauté the shallots, garlic, and ginger until soft, about 5 minutes. Add the wine, water, and salt and bring to a boil. Transfer to a fondue pot and bring the broth to a simmer. Skewer the seafood on fondue forks and cook until just no longer opaque, about 2 minutes. Dip into the sauces.

MAKES 4 TO 6 SERVINGS

Salmon Dinner in a Pot

Tasty chunks of salmon and tofu intermingle with vegetables in this delicious one-pot meal. If you would like to make the meal more substantial, heat cooked udon noodles in the broth after the salmon and vegetables are finished.

LEMON–SOY CONDIMENT

½ cup soy sauce

¼ cup freshly squeezed lemon juice

Sea salt

1½ pounds boneless, skinless salmon fillets, cut into 1-inch cubes

2 leeks (white part only), thinly sliced

3 cups baby spinach leaves

1 pound firm tofu, cut into 1-inch cubes

4 cups water

1 cup dry white wine, such as Sauvignon Blanc

1 small dried red pepper or ⅛ teaspoon cayenne pepper

¾ cup finely grated peeled daikon radish or turnip

4 green onions (including tops), finely chopped

To prepare the lemon-soy condiment: In a small pitcher, stir together the soy sauce and lemon juice and mix thoroughly.

Lightly salt the salmon and arrange on a platter at the table with the leeks, spinach, and tofu. In a fondue pot, bring the water, wine, and red pepper to a boil, then reduce the heat to a gentle simmer. Season with salt to taste. Provide each diner with a soup bowl.

Cook the ingredients in two or three batches as follows: Cook the salmon and leeks for 2 minutes. Then add the spinach and tofu and cook for another 1 to 2 minutes. Diners transfer individual portions to their bowls, add a spoonful of the lemon-soy condiment, and sprinkle a spoonful of grated daikon and green onion on top.

MAKES 4 SERVINGS

Japanese Tempura, Fondue Style

Many of us have eaten these classic Japanese fritters as appetizers, but cooked in the fondue pot, tempura also makes a stellar main course. For each guest, you will want about 6 to 8 ounces of seafood and 8 ounces of assorted vegetables.

12 medium raw shrimp, peeled and deveined

12 sea scallops

6 ounces boneless, skinless firm white fish, such as halibut or sea bass, cut into 2-inch pieces

1 squid, cleaned and cut into 1-inch strips (optional)

8 ounces asparagus, cut diagonally into 1½-inch lengths

1 green or yellow zucchini, cut diagonally into ¼-inch lengths

16 snow peas, ends trimmed

8 small white or brown cremini mushrooms, trimmed

1 red bell pepper, halved, seeded, deribbed, and cut into ½-inch strips

Canola or peanut oil for the fondue pot

TEMPURA BATTER
2 cups all-purpose flour

½ teaspoon salt

¼ teaspoon baking soda

2 large egg yolks

1½ cups ice water

CONDIMENTS AND SUGGESTED SAUCES
Pickled ginger (about ¼ cup), Ponzu (page 72), Soy-Wasabi Sauce (page 70), Sesame-Cilantro Sauce (page 70), and/or Tomato Cocktail Sauce (page 67)

Arrange the seafood and vegetables on a platter at the table, and set out the sauces and pickled ginger in small bowls.

To make the batter: In a medium bowl, stir together the flour, salt, and baking soda. In a separate medium bowl, whisk the egg yolks together with the ice water. Then whisk the egg mixture into the flour mixture. Set the bowl of batter on the table with the seafood and vegetables. Provide each diner with a pair of heat-proof chopsticks.

Fill a metal fondue pot one-third full with oil and heat the oil to 375°F, or until a cube of bread browns in 30 seconds. Diners dip a piece of seafood or vegetable into the batter, then drop it gently into the hot oil. When the batter is creamy or pale beige—not golden brown—it is ready. Have diners dab the fried food onto a paper towel to drain off the excess oil, then dip it into the sauces. Accompany with pickled ginger.

MAKES 4 SERVINGS

Seafood Fondue

Succulent bitefuls of seared shellfish create a delectable feast for a special occasion. A Caesar salad, crusty rolls, steamed artichokes, and a fresh berry or lemon tart would complement this feast.

¾ pound medium raw shrimp, peeled and deveined

¾ pound sea scallops or firm-fleshed boneless, skinless fish, such as halibut, cut into 1-inch chunks

½ pound raw oysters, rinsed

Lemon wedges for garnish

Canola or peanut oil for the fondue pot

SUGGESTED SAUCES
Sour Cream–Dill Sauce (page 67), Tarragon Mustard-Mayonnaise (page 73), Thousand Island Sauce (page 75), and/or Tomato Cocktail Sauce (page 67)

Arrange the shrimp, scallops, oysters, and lemon wedges on a platter at the table, and set out the sauces in small bowls.

Fill a metal fondue pot one-third full with oil and heat the oil to 375°F, or until a cube of bread browns in 30 seconds. With fondue forks or heat-proof chopsticks, cook the shrimp until it turns pink, 1 to 2 minutes. Cook the scallops or fish and oysters until just no longer opaque, 1 to 2 minutes. Dip into the sauces. Garnish with lemon wedges.

MAKES 4 SERVINGS

Chicken and Baby Vegetables in Broth

This is a lovely, convivial entrée in spring, when baby vegetables first arrive in the marketplace. A wide assortment makes a striking array on the table, all ready for dunking in the steaming broth. You might serve a bowl of cooked quinoa alongside.

8 baby carrots, cut into 1-inch pieces

8 Red Bliss or Yukon Gold new potatoes, halved

1½ pounds boneless, skinless chicken breasts

¼ pound sugar peas

8 small yellow pattypan squash, cut into 1-inch pieces

12 small mushroom caps, halved

8 asparagus spears, woody ends snapped off and tops cut into 2-inch lengths

12 snow peas, ends trimmed

3½ cups chicken broth

½ cup dry white wine, such as Sauvignon Blanc

1 green onion (including top), chopped

1 tablespoon snipped fresh tarragon or 1 teaspoon dried tarragon, crushed

SUGGESTED SAUCES
Sour Cream–Dill Sauce (page 67), Aioli (page 68), Rémoulade Sauce (page 68), Tarragon-Mustard Mayonnaise (page 73), and/or Blender Hollandaise Sauce (page 66)

Bring a large pot of water to a boil over high heat. Add the carrots and potatoes and blanch for 5 minutes. Drain, rinse under cold running water, and chill in the refrigerator until ready to use. Cut the chicken into ⅜-by-1½-inch pieces. Arrange the chicken and carrots, potatoes, sugar peas, squash, mushrooms, asparagus, and snow peas on a platter at the table, and set out the sauces in small bowls. Provide each diner with a soup bowl.

In a fondue pot, stir together the broth, wine, green onion, and tarragon. Bring to a gentle boil. Spear the chicken and vegetables onto fondue forks and dip into the broth. Cook the vegetables for 2 minutes and the chicken until no longer pink inside, about 2 minutes. Dip the cooked morsels into the sauces. When all the diners have had their fill of the vegetables and chicken, ladle the broth into the bowls for sipping.

MAKES 4 SERVINGS

SAUCES

TO ADD SPECIAL FILLIP TO AN ENTRÈE FONDUE, DIP THE

meats and vegetables into a zestful sauce. The sauces in this chapter stir together in a jiffy and bring a new dimension to each bite. Herbs, spices, sesame oil, and other condiments spark up such staples as sour cream, mayonnaise, soy, and ketchup. Other ready-to-serve condiments from the pantry, such as chutney, mustard, hoisin sauce, steak sauce, pesto, and balsamic vinegar also work well. If the sauce is particularly runny, you might want to serve it in small, individual bowls.

Chutney-Curry Sauce

Serve this spice-drenched sauce with robust meats such as lamb and pork.

2 teaspoons butter or canola oil

2 shallots, finely chopped

2 teaspoons curry powder

1 cup regular or reduced-fat (not nonfat) sour cream

2 tablespoons finely minced Major Grey's chutney

In a small skillet, heat the butter over medium heat and sauté the shallots until soft, about 3 minutes. Add the curry powder and sauté until the raw taste of the spices is eliminated, about 2 minutes. Let cool. In a small bowl, stir the shallot mixture into the sour cream along with the chutney. Cover and refrigerate until ready to serve, up to 5 days.

MAKES ABOUT 1 CUP

Horseradish–Sour Cream Sauce

This quick-to-assemble sauce is excellent with beef and pork, particularly Beef Bourguignonne Fondue (page 40).

1 cup regular or reduced-fat (not nonfat) sour cream

2 to 3 tablespoons prepared horseradish

1 teaspoon Dijon mustard

1 teaspoon balsamic vinegar

Salt and white pepper

In a small bowl, stir together the sour cream, horseradish, mustard, and vinegar. Season with salt and white pepper to taste. Cover and refrigerate until ready to serve, up to 4 days.

MAKES ABOUT 1¼ CUPS

Blender Hollandaise Sauce

Use a blender to swiftly make a silken, buttery hollandaise that is excellent with vegetables and seafood.

3 large egg yolks

2 tablespoons freshly squeezed
  lemon juice

¼ teaspoon dry mustard

¾ cup (1½ sticks) butter, melted
  and kept warm

Salt and white pepper

Dash of freshly grated nutmeg

In a blender, add the egg yolks, lemon juice, and mustard. Blend until smooth. With the blender running, slowly pour the warm butter in a steady stream into the yolk mixture until emulsified. Season with salt and white pepper to taste and add nutmeg. Serve warm or at room temperature. The sauce will keep, refrigerated, for up to 5 days.

MAKES ABOUT 1 CUP

Béarnaise Sauce

This variation on Hollandaise Sauce (above) enhances beef and lamb.

2 sprigs parsley

2 shallots, finely chopped

¼ cup tarragon vinegar

1 cup Blender Hollandaise
  Sauce (recipe above)

2 teaspoons minced fresh tarragon or
  ½ teaspoon dried tarragon

⅛ teaspoon cayenne pepper (optional)

In a small saucepan over medium-high heat, bring the parsley, shallots, and vinegar to a boil and reduce to 1 tablespoon liquid. Remove from the heat and allow to cool. Add the cooled, reduced liquid to the hollandaise sauce and stir to blend. Stir in the tarragon and cayenne pepper, if using. Cover and refrigerate until ready to serve, up to 5 days.

MAKES ABOUT 1 CUP

Tomato Cocktail Sauce

This classic sauce will please all ages. It complements seafood beautifully.

⅔ cup ketchup

⅓ cup chili sauce

2 teaspoons Worcestershire sauce

1 tablespoon freshly squeezed lemon juice

Salt and freshly ground black pepper

In a small bowl, stir together the ketchup, chili sauce, Worcestershire sauce, and lemon juice. Season with salt and pepper to taste. Cover and refrigerate until ready to serve, up to 10 days.

MAKES ABOUT 1 CUP

Sour Cream–Dill Sauce

This herb sauce is a natural with seafood and vegetables such as asparagus, fennel, artichokes, and potatoes. Store dill in the refrigerator like a bouquet, the stems immersed in a glass of water and the fronds covered with a plastic bag. It will keep nicely for a week or two.

1 cup regular or reduced-fat (not nonfat) sour cream

¼ cup minced fresh dill

2 cloves garlic, finely chopped

2 tablespoons minced parsley

1 teaspoon freshly squeezed lemon juice

Salt and white pepper

In a small bowl, stir together the sour cream, dill, garlic, parsley, and lemon juice. Season with salt and white pepper to taste. Cover and refrigerate until ready to serve, up to 4 days.

MAKES ABOUT 1¼ CUPS

Aioli

This quick, aromatic sauce is great with lamb and vegetables.

1 cup homemade or commercial
   mayonnaise

3 to 4 cloves garlic, minced

In a blender or food processor, blend the mayonnaise with the garlic until smooth. Cover and refrigerate until ready to serve, up to 10 days.

MAKES ABOUT 1 CUP

Rémoulade Sauce

Capers and herbs enliven this mayonnaise-based sauce, which will give a snappy edge to fish, seafood, and vegetables.

¾ cup homemade or commercial
   mayonnaise

2 tablespoons minced fresh chives

2 tablespoons minced parsley

2 teaspoons finely chopped fresh
   tarragon or ½ teaspoon dried tarragon

2 tablespoons capers, chopped

1 green onion (white part only),
   finely chopped

1 clove garlic, minced

Salt and white pepper

In a small bowl, stir together the mayonnaise, chives, parsley, tarragon, capers, green onion, and garlic. Season with salt and white pepper to taste. Cover and refrigerate until ready to serve, up to 4 days.

MAKES ABOUT 1 CUP

Sesame-Cilantro Sauce

This lively sauce, which takes just a few minutes to assemble, will lend piquancy to seafood and vegetables, in particular asparagus, broccoli, cauliflower, artichoke hearts, sugar peas, and bok choy.

¼ cup freshly squeezed lemon juice

3 tablespoons white wine vinegar

3 tablespoons Asian-style sesame oil

2 tablespoons minced cilantro

1 green onion (white part only), chopped

Salt and freshly ground black pepper

Dash of cayenne pepper

In a small bowl, stir together the lemon juice, vinegar, sesame oil, cilantro, and green onion. Season with salt, black pepper, and cayenne pepper to taste. Cover and refrigerate until ready to serve, up to 5 days.

MAKES ABOUT ¾ CUP SAUCE

Soy-Wasabi Sauce

The kick of wasabi, or Japanese horseradish, gives a lively accent to seafood.

⅓ cup soy sauce

2 teaspoons prepared wasabi paste

In a small bowl, stir together the soy sauce and the wasabi paste. Serve at room temperature. This sauce will keep, refrigerated, for up to 5 days.

MAKES ABOUT ½ CUP

Chile-Peanut Sauce

This spicy peanut sauce lends a vibrancy to many fondues. It complements beef, pork, lamb, duck, and chicken particularly well.

6 tablespoons smooth peanut butter

1 tablespoon soy sauce

1 teaspoon Asian-style sesame oil

2 teaspoons rice wine vinegar

2 teaspoons sugar

2 cloves garlic, minced

⅓ cup water or chicken broth, heated

¼ cup finely chopped cilantro (optional)

5 to 10 drops chile oil

In a small bowl, stir together the peanut butter, soy sauce, sesame oil, vinegar, sugar, and garlic, and whisk in the water or broth, blending until smooth. Stir in the cilantro, if using, and chile oil to taste. If desired, thin the sauce to the desired consistency with a tablespoon or two of additional water or broth. Cover and refrigerate until ready to serve, up to 3 days.

MAKES ABOUT 1 CUP

Ponzu

This sauce is typically served with Shabu-Shabu (page 45). It also goes well with other beef and lamb fondues.

½ cup soy sauce

½ cup freshly squeezed lemon juice

1 tablespoon mirin (Japanese sweet cooking wine)

1 tablespoon chopped green onion, (including tops)

In a small bowl, stir together the soy sauce, lemon juice, mirin, and green onion. Cover and refrigerate until ready to serve, up to 3 days.

MAKES ABOUT 1 CUP

Tarragon-Mustard Mayonnaise

Mayonnaise and sour cream are quickly transformed into appealing sauces. This mixture of mayonnaise with spicy Dijon mustard and aromatic tarragon will uplift chicken, vegetables, and seafood.

½ cup home-made or commercial mayonnaise

⅓ cup regular or reduced-fat (not non-fat) sour cream

2 tablespoons freshly squeezed lemon juice

2 teaspoons minced fresh tarragon or ½ teaspoon dried tarragon

2 teaspoons Dijon mustard

In small bowl, stir together the mayonnaise, sour cream, lemon juice, tarragon, and mustard. Cover and refrigerate until ready to serve, up to 5 days.

MAKES ABOUT 1 CUP

Basil Pesto

This fragrant herb sauce enhances Tuscan Cheese Fondue (page 29) and also serves as a seductive complement to meats and fish.

1 cup packed fresh basil leaves

2 tablespoons pine nuts or shelled pistachios

1 large clove garlic, mashed

2 tablespoons grated Parmesan cheese

3 to 4 tablespoons extra-virgin olive oil

In a blender or food processor fitted with the metal blade, pulse until minced the basil, pine nuts, garlic, and Parmesan cheese. With the motor running, slowly pour the olive oil in a steady stream and process until emulsified. Transfer to a small bowl, cover, and refrigerate, until ready to serve, up to 5 days.

MAKES ABOUT 1 CUP

Teriyaki Sauce

Teriyaki is a versatile sauce that is excellent on poultry, red meat, and seafood.

½ cup soy sauce

1 clove garlic, minced

1 tablespoon packed light brown sugar

1 tablespoon rice wine vinegar

¼ cup sake or pale dry sherry

In a small bowl, stir together the soy sauce, garlic, brown sugar, vinegar, and sake. Cover and refrigerate until ready to serve, up to 10 days.

MAKES ABOUT 1 CUP

Sun-Dried Tomato–Balsamic Sauce

The beloved Italian condiments of sun-dried tomatoes and balsamic vinegar combine beautifully to make a quick sauce for Mediterranean-style fondues with chicken, pork, or beef.

½ cup balsamic vinegar

2 tablespoons extra-virgin olive oil

6 oil-packed sun-dried tomatoes,
  drained and finely chopped

2 tablespoons minced fresh chives

1 clove garlic, minced

In a small bowl, stir together the vinegar, olive oil, tomatoes, chives, and garlic. Cover and let stand until serving time. The sauce will keep, refrigerated, for up to 5 days.

MAKES ABOUT 1 CUP

Yogurt Sauce with Mint, Cilantro, or Oregano

Use different fresh herbs to adapt this tangy, cool sauce to your meal. Mint is delightful with lamb. Oregano is excellent with pork or lamb, and cilantro suits seafood. Greek-style yogurt, with its thicker consistency and fuller flavor, works best, but any unflavored, regular-fat yogurt will substitute.

1 cup Greek-style yogurt

2 tablespoons olive oil

¼ cup minced fresh mint or cilantro leaves or 2 tablespoons minced fresh oregano

1 tablespoon freshly squeezed lemon juice

1 clove garlic, minced

Salt and freshly ground black pepper

In a small bowl, stir together the yogurt, olive oil, herb of your choice, lemon juice, and garlic. Season with salt and pepper to taste. Cover and refrigerate until ready to serve, up to 4 days.

MAKES ABOUT 1¼ CUPS

Thousand Island Sauce

The excellent Louis Dressing makes a superb sauce with fish, seafood, and vegetables.

½ cup home-made or commercial mayonnaise

¼ cup chile sauce

1 shallot or green onion (white part only) finely chopped

1 tablespoon chopped red or green bell pepper

Salt and white pepper

In a small bowl, stir together the mayonnaise, chile sauce, shallot or onion, and red or green bell pepper. Season with salt and white pepper to taste. Cover and refrigerate until ready to serve, up to 3 days.

MAKES ABOUT ¾ CUP

DESSERT
FONDUES

DIP INTO A CHOCOLATE, BUTTERSCOTCH, OR FRUIT FONDUE

for a luscious finale to dinner. Dessert fondues will delight all your guests and bring everyone into the conversation for a bit of fun and frivolity.

Dessert fondues can be enhanced with little bowls of special coatings to cloak the fruits or morsels of cake once they are dipped. Chopped toasted almonds, pecans, and hazelnuts add a wonderful flourish, as do grated bittersweet or milk chocolate, praline, and toasted shredded coconut.

Select a high-quality chocolate such as Guittard, Valrhona, or Scharffen Berger. Chop chocolate bars with a cook's knife into small pieces before melting. Use low heat as chocolate melts at body temperature and scorches easily.

Chocolate-Orange Fondue

Fragrant orange zest and orange-flavored Grand Marnier pair naturally with chocolate to create this luscious dipping sauce. Light, crisp ladyfinger cookies, amaretti cookies (available at any Italian foods store), or even biscotti make sophisticated dippers.

10 ounces bittersweet or semisweet chocolate

⅔ cup half-and-half

1 teaspoon finely grated orange zest

2 to 3 tablespoons Grand Marnier

DIPPERS
Ladyfinger cookies, amaretti cookies, and/or biscotti

Cut the chocolate into ½-inch pieces. In a fondue pot over low heat, combine the chocolate, half-and-half, and orange zest. Stir until the chocolate is melted and the mixture is smooth. Stir in the Grand Marnier. Keep warm over low heat.

Arrange the dippers on a serving platter and set it next to the fondue pot so guests can swirl the cookies in the warm sauce.

MAKES 2 CUPS, OR 6 SERVINGS

Classic Chocolate Fondue

Top-quality chocolate provides an elegant richness to this ever-popular dessert fondue, whose character can be altered subtly with your choice of spirits. Serve chocolate fondue with a mix of fruits and squares of angel food cake or pound cake. Or, for a divine treat, offer tiny frozen cream puffs filled with ice cream. Remember to set the fondue over low heat so the chocolate does not scorch. This recipe makes a thick sauce; if desired, thin it with an extra tablespoon or two of cream.

10 ounces bittersweet or semisweet
  chocolate

⅔ cup heavy (whipping) cream

2 tablespoons rum, kirsch, Kahlúa,
  or Cognac

DIPPERS
Strawberries; banana chunks;
mandarin orange segments; pineapple
chunks; angel food cake or pound
cake, cut into 1-inch cubes; and/or
1-inch cream puffs, filled with vanilla
ice cream and frozen hard

Cut the chocolate into ½-inch pieces. In a fondue pot over low heat, combine the chocolate, cream, and rum. Stir until the chocolate is melted and the mixture is smooth. Keep warm over low heat.

Arrange the dippers on a serving platter and set it next to the fondue pot. Spear the morsels with fondue forks and swirl them in the warm sauce.

MAKES 1¾ CUPS, OR 6 SERVINGS

Cappuccino Fondue

Chocolate, coffee, and cinnamon intertwine in this enticing fondue. Provide assorted sweets—marshmallows, doughnut chunks, or spicy coffeecake cubes—for swirling in the warm sauce.

6 ounces milk chocolate

4 ounces bittersweet chocolate

¾ cup plus 2 tablespoons half-and-half

2 teaspoons instant espresso powder

¼ teaspoon ground cinnamon

DIPPERS
Cinnamon coffeecake, cut into
1-inch cubes; fruitcake, sliced thinly;
marshmallows; doughnut chunks; and/or
gingerbread, cut into 1-inch cubes

Cut the chocolates into ½-inch pieces. In a fondue pot over low heat, combine the chocolates, half-and-half, espresso powder, and cinnamon. Stir until the chocolate is melted and the mixture is smooth. Keep warm over low heat.

Arrange the dippers on a serving platter and set it next to the fondue pot. Spear the morsels with fondue forks and swirl them in the warm sauce.

MAKES 1½ CUPS, OR 4 TO 6 SERVINGS

White Chocolate–Almond Fondue

Finely chopped toasted almonds provide a special flavor in this snowy white fondue. Mexican wedding cookies are butter-powdered sugar cookies dotted with chopped pecans or almonds. Banana slices and Mexican wedding cookies were the tasters' top favorites for dipping.

½ cup raw whole almonds

8 ounces white chocolate

4 tablespoons heavy (whipping) cream

2 tablespoons light corn syrup

1 to 2 tablespoons amaretto or Cognac

½ teaspoon vanilla extract

DIPPERS
Strawberries; pineapple chunks; kiwi fruit slices; banana slices; carambola slices; papaya slices; Mexican wedding cookies; and/or chocolate brownies, cut into 1-inch cubes

Preheat the oven to 350°F. Put the almonds in a baking pan and bake in the oven until toasted, 8 to 10 minutes. Let cool a few minutes. Chop the nuts finely.

Chop the white chocolate finely. In the top of a double boiler set over simmering water, combine the chocolate, cream, and corn syrup. Stir until the chocolate is melted and the mixture is smooth. Stir in the amaretto, vanilla, and chopped almonds. Transfer to a fondue pot and keep warm over low heat.

Arrange the fruit and cookie dippers on a serving platter and set it next to the fondue pot. Spear the morsels with fondue forks and swirl them in the warm sauce.

MAKES 2¼ CUPS, OR 6 SERVINGS

Chocolate-Hazelnut Fondue

Toasted hazelnuts and a splash of nut-flavored liqueur make a lovely complement to satiny melted chocolate. Dried fruit—apricots, pears, and plums—and crisp fresh apple slices make an enticing sweet-tart backdrop for a chocolate coating.

⅓ cup whole hazelnuts

8 ounces bittersweet or semisweet chocolate

½ cup half-and-half or heavy (whipping) cream

2 tablespoons Frangelico or amaretto

DIPPERS
Dried apricots, dried pear wedges, dried plums, and/or fresh or dried apple slices

Preheat the oven to 350°F. Put the hazelnuts in a baking pan and bake in the oven until toasted, 8 to 10 minutes. Let cool a few minutes, and then rub between paper towels to remove the skins. Chop the nuts finely.

Cut the chocolate into ½-inch pieces. In a fondue pot set over low heat, combine the chocolate and the half-and-half. Stir until the chocolate is melted and the mixture is smooth. Stir in the Frangelico and chopped nuts. Keep warm over low heat.

Arrange the dippers on a serving platter and set it next to the fondue pot. Spear the fruits with fondue forks and swirl them in the warm sauce.

MAKES 2 CUPS, OR 6 SERVINGS

Chocolate-Peanut Fondue

The crunch of peanuts laces this chocolate fondue, giving fruits and cake a rich textural coating. Peanut butter lovers adore this one.

6 ounces semisweet chocolate, cut into chunks

⅓ cup packed light brown sugar

½ cup milk

½ cup chunky peanut butter

DIPPERS
Marshmallows; tangerine segments; banana slices; apple slices; pear slices; mango chunks; and/or angel food cake or pound cake, cut into 1-inch cubes

In a medium saucepan over medium-low heat, combine the chocolate, brown sugar, and milk. Stir until the chocolate is melted. Add the peanut butter and cook, stirring, until heated through. Transfer to a fondue pot and keep warm over low heat.

Arrange the dippers on a serving platter and set it next to the fondue pot. Spear the dippers with fondue forks and swirl them in the warm sauce.

MAKES 2¼ CUPS, OR 6 SERVINGS

Caramel-Pecan Fondue

Caramelizing sugar develops a rich flavor and deep-brown color in this dessert fondue. To keep the sugar from crystallizing as it caramelizes, swirl and shake the pan in the beginning until the sugar dissolves.

½ cup raw pecans

1 cup sugar

¼ cup water

½ cup (1 stick) unsalted butter

½ cup half-and-half or heavy (whipping) cream

½ teaspoon vanilla extract

DIPPERS
Strawberries, banana chunks, pineapple chunks, mango chunks, peach slices, and/or kiwi fruit quarters

Preheat the oven to 350°F. Put the pecans in a baking pan and bake in the oven until toasted, 8 to 10 minutes. Let cool a few minutes. Chop the nuts finely.

In a medium saucepan over medium-high heat, combine the sugar and water and heat, shaking and swirling the pan without letting the sugar-water boil, until the sugar dissolves. Bring the mixture to a boil, cover, and cook for 1 minute. Remove the cover and boil until the syrup develops a rich, golden color. Remove from the heat and quickly add the butter, stirring until it melts. Stir in the half-and-half and vanilla. Transfer to a fondue pot and keep warm over low heat.

Arrange the fruit dippers on a serving platter and set it next to the fondue pot. Spear the dippers with fondue forks and swirl them in the warm sauce.

MAKES 2¼ CUPS, OR 6 SERVINGS

Butterscotch Fondue

Fresh, juicy fruit makes a superb contrast to this caramel-like brown-sugar sauce.

½ cup (1 stick) unsalted butter

1 cup firmly packed light brown sugar

½ cup heavy (whipping) cream

¼ cup light corn syrup

⅛ teaspoon freshly squeezed
  lemon juice

2 tablespoons Cognac (optional)

DIPPERS
Strawberries, banana chunks,
pineapple chunks, peach slices,
and/or kiwi fruit slices

In a medium saucepan over medium heat, melt the butter and stir in the brown sugar, cream, corn syrup, and lemon juice. Bring to a boil, reduce the heat, and simmer for 5 minutes, stirring constantly. Stir in the Cognac, if using, and transfer to a fondue pot. Keep warm over low heat.

Arrange the fruit dippers on a serving platter and set it next to the fondue pot. Spear the fruit pieces with fondue forks and swirl them in the warm sauce.

MAKES 2 CUPS, OR 6 SERVINGS

Blackberry-Balsamic Fondue

A splash of brandy and well-aged balsamic vinegar intensify the fruity flavor of this midnight-blue fondue. It is ideal with small bites of cake or nutty cookies. You can find aged balsamic vinegar at gourmet foods stores; it has a much richer flavor than standard commercial varieties.

½ cup sugar

½ cup water

3 cups fresh or frozen blackberries

2 tablespoons 10-year-old balsamic vinegar

2 tablespoons freshly squeezed lemon juice

2 tablespoons brandy (optional)

DIPPERS
Brownies, angel food cake, sweet brioche, sponge cake, or pound cake, cut into 1-inch cubes; and/or small macaroons

In a medium saucepan over medium heat, combine the sugar and water and bring to a boil. Reduce the heat and simmer for 3 minutes. Add the berries and vinegar and simmer until the berries are soft, 2 to 3 minutes. Let cool, then strain into a medium bowl through a fine-mesh sieve, pressing the berries with the back of a spoon to extract all the juice. Stir in the lemon juice and brandy, if using. Transfer to a fondue pot over low heat and heat until the sauce is hot. Keep warm.

Arrange the dippers on a serving platter and set it next to the fondue pot. Spear the brownies, cake, and macaroons with fondue forks and swirl them in the warm sauce.

MAKES 2½ CUPS, OR 6 SERVINGS

Candied Ginger, Lemon, and Cream Cheese Fondue

Tropical fruits are lovely dipped in this creamy, ginger-sparked fondue.

6 tablespoons half-and-half

8 ounces regular (not reduced-fat)
   cream cheese, cut into ½-inch cubes

3 tablespoons honey

2 teaspoons grated lemon zest

2 tablespoons freshly squeezed
   lemon juice

¼ cup minced crystallized ginger

DIPPERS
Pineapple chunks; mango chunks;
papaya chunks; tangerine segments;
kiwi fruit wedges; strawberries; and/or
angel food cake or sponge cake, cut
into 1-inch cubes

In a fondue pot over low heat, heat the half-and-half until steaming. Add the cream cheese and stir until completely melted. Stir in the honey, lemon zest, lemon juice, and ginger. Keep warm over low heat.

Arrange the dippers on a serving platter and set it next to the fondue pot. Spear the fruit and cake with fondue forks and swirl them in the warm sauce.

MAKES 1½ CUPS, OR 4 TO 6 SERVINGS

Raspberry Fondue

This ruby-hued berry fondue makes a brilliant coating for angel food cake, pound cake, or small macaroons. Amaretti are crisp, airy macaroons flavored with almond or apricot kernel paste. Framboise, a French raspberry-flavored liqueur, will amplify the fruity character of the sauce even more.

2½ cups fresh or frozen raspberries,
   at room temperature

⅓ cup red currant jelly

3 tablespoons sugar

2 teaspoons cornstarch blended
   with 1 tablespoon cold water

2 tablespoons framboise or
   orange liqueur

DIPPERS
Angel food cake or pound cake, cut
into 1-inch cubes; small macaroons;
and/or amaretti cookies

Purée the raspberries in a blender and press through a fine-mesh sieve into a medium bowl, discarding the seeds. In a small saucepan over medium heat, combine the purée and the jelly and bring to a boil. Stir in the sugar, reduce the heat, and simmer for 1 minute. Slowly add the cornstarch mixture to the raspberry mixture and cook, stirring, until thickened. Stir in the framboise and transfer to a fondue pot. Keep warm over low heat.

Arrange the cake and cookie dippers on a serving platter and set it next to the fondue pot. Spear the morsels on fondue forks and swirl them in the warm sauce.

MAKES 1½ CUPS, OR 4 TO 6 SERVINGS

INDEX